THE MISSING DINOSAUR

D1524479

Written by Abraham Erickson

Illustrated by Ian Gibson

J4A Publishing LLC
4445 Corporation Ln, Ste 264
Virginia Beach, VA 23462

To my children, who continue to inspire me to believe.

SMACK.

The lid to the wood toy chest cracked as it fell shut.

"Dad, I can't find it."

Alex's favorite toy, a Tyrannosaurus Rex, was missing.

"Did you look in the bathtub?" I asked.

At three years old, Alex had mastered pronouncing most dinosaur names. He was saying Pachycephalosaurus before he could say Daddy.

430

Title	The Missing Dinosaur
Condition	Good
Location	Zone A Row 1 Bay 1 Shelf 3 Item 430
Description	Fast Shipping - Safe and Secure Mailer! This purchase benefits the Rappahannock Goodwill Industries. Thank you for supporting our mission.
Source	General
SKU	3YGW6Z0002WP
ASIN	B0CNB2D6LH
Code	9798867408954
Employee	thrown
Date Arrived	9/4/2024 9:56:03 AM

430

"He's not there, either," Alex said.

"OK, we'll find him. You look under the kitchen table and I'll check around the TV stand."

T-Rex won all the battles, and it was time to fight again. An alliance between Ankylosaurus, Brachiosaurus, and Velociraptors threatened the villagers.

But the King of the Dinosaurs was missing.

"Alex, any luck?"

"He's lost. I'll never find him." Alex had been sad before, but this was different.

This was loss. This was heartache.

"Alexander, when you need help pray to Heavenly Father. He is listening to you. He will answer your prayers. He will help you find your missing dinosaur."

Despair turned to determination in his eyes and Alex began to pray.

"Heavenly Father, I can't find T-Rex. Please help me find him. In the name of Jesus Christ, amen."

Alex stood up and continued his search.

We prayed often as a family. We gave thanks for food. We prayed before bed. We prayed for a good day. But now the pressure was on. Alex needs help, and I told him to trust God... to find a toy.

As I watched Little Man look for T-Rex, I couldn't have been more proud. I hoped my faith could equal that of my son's.

"Please, Father," I prayed silently in my heart, "bless this teaching opportunity. Please answer Alex's prayer."

At this moment an impression came to my mind, "Look behind the TV stand."

I had looked there moments before, but there was no sign of T-Rex.

Acting on the prompting, I reached behind the stand, but felt nothing. I reached a little further. There was a gap between the back of the stand and the floor.

And there it was.

"Guess what, Alex? Look what I found!"

His smile said it all. He was filled with joy; I was filled with relief. We were both grateful.

"Now son, you need to thank God for answering your prayer, and helping you find your favorite toy." Alex offered a short, sweet prayer of Thanksgiving, then they were off.

Alex rushed T-Rex to the fight before it was too late. The villagers were saved.

Made in the USA
Middletown, DE
21 November 2023

43143142R00018